TEAM SPIRIT®

SMART BOOKS FOR YOUNG FANS

THE PITTSBURGH PIRATES

BY
MARK STEWART

NORWOODHOUSE PRESS
CHICAGO, ILLINOIS

Norwood House Press
P.O. Box 316598
Chicago, Illinois 60631

For information regarding Norwood House Press, please visit our website at:
www.norwoodhousepress.com or call 866-565-2900.

All photos courtesy of Getty Images except the following:
Tom DiPace (4, 11, 14), Author's Collection (6, 9, 24, 33, 42 bottom, 43 bottom),
Macfadden Publications (7), SportsChrome (10), Sports Champions, Inc. (15),
Turkey Red (16), Goudey Gum Co. (17 top),
Topps, Inc. (17 bottom, 23, 35 top left, 37, 38, 40, 41, 42 top left, 43 bottom right, 45),
Gum, Inc. (20, 34 bottom right), Exhibit Supply Co. (22), Black Book Partners Archives (25, 42 bottom left),
TCMA, Ltd. (26), Sweet Caporal (28), Fan Craze Company (34 top), Old Judge & Gypsy Queen (34 bottom left),
Leading Magazine Corp. (36), Fleer Corp. (39), Bowman Gum Co. (43 top right), Matt Richman (48).
Cover Photo: John Grieshop

The memorabilia and artifacts pictured in this book are presented for educational and informational purposes,
and come from the collection of the author.

Editor: Mike Kennedy
Designer: Ron Jaffe
Project Management: Black Book Partners, LLC.
Special thanks to Topps, Inc.

Library of Congress Cataloging-in-Publication Data

Stewart, Mark, 1960-
  The Pittsburgh Pirates / by Mark Stewart.
      p. cm. -- (Team spirit)
  Includes bibliographical references and index.
  Summary: "A Team Spirit Baseball edition featuring the Pittsburgh Pirates
that chronicles the history and accomplishments of the team. Includes access
to the Team Spirit website, which provides additional information, updates
and photos"--Provided by publisher.
  ISBN 978-1-59953-493-0 (library : alk. paper) -- ISBN 978-1-60357-373-3
(ebook) 1. Pittsburgh Pirates (Baseball team)--History--Juvenile
literature. I. Title.
  GV875.P5S837 2012
  796.357'640974886--dc23
                                            2011047976

Manufactured in the United States of America in North Mankato, Minnesota.
196N—012012

COVER PHOTO: The Pirates celebrate a win on their home field.

TABLE OF CONTENTS

ABOUT OUR GLOSSARY

In this book, there may be several words that you are reading for the first time. Some are sports words, some are new vocabulary words, and some are familiar words that are used in an unusual way. All of these words are defined on page 46. Throughout the book, sports words appear in **bold type**. Regular vocabulary words appear in ***bold italic type***.

MEET THE PIRATES

There is an old baseball saying that goes, "Good pitching stops good hitting." That may be true for most teams, but it's usually the other way around with the Pittsburgh Pirates. For *generations*, they have been among baseball's best-hitting teams. Pittsburgh has a proud *tradition* of batting champions and league-leading home run hitters.

Of course, it also takes good pitching and defense to win championships. When the Pirates have been able to put all of these pieces together, they have been unbeatable. Even if Pittsburgh doesn't win a championship, the team plays exciting baseball and never gives up.

This book tells the story of the Pirates. They have given baseball some of its greatest moments and most unforgettable players. Pittsburgh plays to win from the beginning of the season to the end. When you wear the team's black and gold uniform, you are expected to do nothing less.

Jose Tabata congratulates Pedro Alvarez after a home run.

GLORY DAYS

Pittsburgh joined the **National League (NL)** in 1887. The club was originally called the Alleghenys. They actually played their first game five years earlier, in 1882. That season, Pittsburgh became a member of the **American Association (AA)**, a rival league to the NL.

The team's best player was Ed Swartwood. He won the AA batting crown in 1883.

By 1900, Barney Dreyfuss had bought the Pittsburgh club. The team was now known as the Pirates, though the name wasn't originally meant as a compliment. Pittsburgh got the nickname after people accused the club of "stealing" a player from another team.

Dreyfuss was a smart businessman. He also owned an NL team in Louisville, Kentucky. Dreyfuss decided to shut down that club, but first he traded his best players to Pittsburgh. Included in that deal were outfielder Fred Clarke and shortstop Honus Wagner, the game's greatest young star.

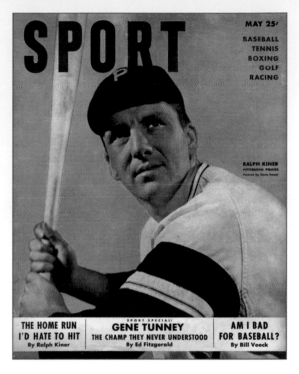

The Pirates won the **pennant** three years in a row starting in 1901. In 1903, they played in the first modern **World Series** and lost to the **American League (AL)** champions from Boston. Six years later, Pittsburgh won the championship. That team defeated the Detroit Tigers in a showdown between Wagner and Ty Cobb, the AL's best player.

The Pirates took the NL pennant again in 1925 and 1927. Those clubs had strong hitters, including Pie Traynor, Kiki Cuyler, and Glenn Wright, and later the Waner brothers, Paul and Lloyd. Pittsburgh finished in second place five times in the years that followed, but the team did not return to the World Series. The Pirates sank to the bottom of the league in the 1950s. The only reason many fans came to the ballpark was to watch the amazing power hitting of Ralph Kiner.

LEFT: Honus Wagner slides home safely. He was the NL's best player in the early 1900s.   **ABOVE**: Slugger Ralph Kiner appeared on a lot of magazine covers in the 1950s.

By the 1960s, the Pirates had rebuilt their club around good pitching and defense. Vern Law, Bob Friend, and Roy Face were among the top pitchers in the league. Roberto Clemente, Bill Virdon, Dick Groat, and Bill Mazeroski were excellent fielders and provided dependable hitting. The Pirates won the World Series in 1960 and had several more winning seasons during the *decade*. In 1971, Clemente led a new group of stars to another pennant. He teamed with Willie Stargell, Manny Sanguillen, Dave Cash, Richie Hebner, and Al Oliver to bring a fourth championship to Pittsburgh.

In 1979, it was Stargell's turn to lead the team to the World Series. Known to his younger teammates as "Pops," he played like a kid, and his enthusiasm rubbed off on the Pirates and their fans. With help from Bill Madlock and Dave Parker, Pittsburgh danced its way to the championship to the beat of a popular disco song called "We Are Family."

During the 1980s and 1990s, building a winning team became more difficult for the Pirates. They could not match the money

LEFT: Roberto Clemente
ABOVE: Willie Stargell

that other teams spent on players. But thanks to a clever manager named Jim Leyland, Pittsburgh still competed with the top teams in baseball. Players such as Doug Drabek, John Smiley, Bobby Bonilla, Jay Bell, Andy Van Slyke, and Barry Bonds developed into **All-Stars**. Leyland knew how to get the best out of every player on the team. The Pirates came within one out of reaching the World Series in 1992.

Unfortunately, Pittsburgh was unable to keep this core of players together. The club had no choice but to rebuild for the 21st century. The Pirates did a good job picking young hitters. Among the exciting players who wore the Pittsburgh uniform were Jason Kendall, Brian Giles, Jason Bay, Freddy Sanchez, Aramis Ramirez, and Adam LaRoche. Kendall was an All-Star three times. Giles hit 165 home runs in five seasons. In 2004, Jason Bay was the NL's best **rookie**.

The problem for Pittsburgh was pitching. The Pirates couldn't find the type of arms that had helped them win championships decades earlier.

In 2011, fans noticed something different about their team. A new generation of stars had taken over, and a new manager convinced them they could be winners. Manager Clint Hurdle worked endless hours with young hitters Andrew McCutchen, Jose Tabata, Neil Walker, and Pedro Alvarez. He also taught young pitchers Charlie Morton, James McDonald, and Joel Hanrahan what it takes to win.

In July of 2011, something amazing happened. The Pirates found themselves in first place. Pittsburgh caught baseball fever. The players believed they could beat anyone. Although the Pirates fell short of winning the **NL Central** crown, the other teams in the division knew that their day was coming. Pittsburgh fans knew it, too.

LEFT: Barry Bonds
ABOVE: Andrew McCutchen

HOME TURF

For more than 60 years, the Pirates played in Forbes Field. The ballpark was named after a general who had won important battles near Pittsburgh in the 1700s. The outfield walls were far away from home plate, so players found it hard to hit home runs. The Pirates moved to Three Rivers Stadium in 1970. It was built in a spot where three rivers—the Monongahela, Allegheny, and Ohio—come together.

After 31 seasons there, the team moved to a new ballpark on the Allegheny River. It has beautiful arches like Forbes Field, plus great views of the Pittsburgh skyline and waterfront. Right field is special territory. The wall is 21 feet high in honor of Roberto Clemente, who wore uniform #21.

BY THE NUMBERS

- The Pirates' stadium has 38,362 seats.
- The distance from home plate to the left field foul pole is 325 feet.
- The distance from home plate to the center field fence is 399 feet.
- The distance from home plate to the right field foul pole is 320 feet.

The stands are full for the 2006 All-Star Game at the Pirates' ballpark.

Back when the team was called the Alleghenys, the players wore striped uniforms. Their fans called them the "Potato Bugs," after a brightly striped insect. In the first half of the 1900s, after the team became the Pirates, Pittsburgh's main color was dark blue, often with red trim added.

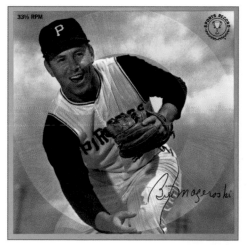

The Pirates started wearing their familiar black and gold colors in 1948. In 1957, they switched to a uniform with a sleeveless jersey. The team kept that style right through the 1960s.

In the 1970s, the Pirates changed back to a regular uniform, but they used many different combinations of black, gold, and white. At times, they also wore black and gold *pinstripes*. Today, the Pirates feature several different styles, including a "throwback" look that has a *P* on the front of the jersey.

LEFT: Neil Walker models the team's 2011 road uniform.
ABOVE: Bill Mazeroski poses in the sleeveless jersey of the 1960s.

The Pirates played in the first modern World Series in 1903. Many of their stars were injured, and they lost to the Boston Americans. Pittsburgh fans were eager for their team to challenge again for a championship. They got their wish in 1909.

CAMNITZ Pittsburg

The Pirates won the pennant easily that season, thanks to their great star Honus Wagner. He led the NL in batting for the fourth year in a row and was the only player in the league to reach 100 **runs batted in (RBIs)**. **Player-manager** Fred Clarke and outfielder Tommy Leach scored many of those runs. Howie Camnitz, Vic Willis, and Babe Adams were the team's best pitchers. In the World Series, Pittsburgh beat the Detroit Tigers for the championship.

The Pirates returned to the World Series in 1925, against the Washington Senators. It took seven games to decide the winner. Pittsburgh was led by two speedy outfielders, Max Carey and

Harold "Pie" Traynor

LEFT: Howie Camnitz won 25 games for the Pirates in 1909.
RIGHT: Pie Traynor helped the Pirates win two pennants.
BELOW: A trading card shows the celebration after the 1960 World Series.

Kiki Cuyler, and hard-hitting infielders Pie Traynor and Glenn Wright. The Pirates lost three of the first four games but fought back to tie the series. In Game 7, they were behind until the seventh inning. Traynor tied the game with a triple. Two innings later, Cuyler drove home the winning runs.

The Pirates played in the World Series again in 1927, but they were swept by the powerful New York Yankees. Pittsburgh fans had to wait until 1960 for their next chance at a title. The Pirates faced

1960 WORLD SERIES

The Winners Celebrate

the Yankees again, but this time they beat New York in seven wild games. Shortstop Dick Groat, outfielder Roberto Clemente, and pitchers Vern Law and Roy Face starred for the Pirates. The winning hit came with

the score tied 9–9 in the bottom of the ninth inning of Game 7. Bill Mazeroski drove a ball over the left field wall to give Pittsburgh a dramatic victory.

The Pirates won championships again in 1971 and 1979. Both times they played the Baltimore Orioles, and both times Pittsburgh trailed in the series. In 1971, Clemente and pitcher Steve Blass led their comeback. Blass beat Baltimore 2–1 in Game 7. Clemente sparked the offense and gave the Pirates the runs they needed to secure the victory.

In 1979, slugger Willie Stargell and relief pitcher Kent Tekulve helped the Pirates win the World Series in seven games. The team also got great pitching from Bert Blyleven and John Candelaria. For the second time in their history, the Pirates won the championship after trailing three games to one.

ABOVE: Steve Blass pitches in the 1971 World Series.
RIGHT: Willie Stargell rounds third base after hitting a home run in Game 7 of the 1979 World Series.

GO-TO GUYS

To be a true star in baseball, you need more than a quick bat and a strong arm. You have to be a "go-to guy"—someone the manager wants on the pitcher's mound or in the batter's box when it matters most. Fans of the Pirates have had a lot to cheer about over the years, including these great stars ...

THE PIONEERS

HONUS WAGNER   Shortstop

• BORN: 2/24/1874 • DIED: 12/6/1955 • PLAYED FOR TEAM: 1900 TO 1917
Honus Wagner was a powerful hitter, fast runner, and excellent fielder—and the best player in the NL in the early 1900s. Wagner, who won eight batting championships, loved baseball so much that he continued to play for local teams in Pittsburgh until he was 50.

"ARKY" VAUGHAN

ARKY VAUGHAN   Shortstop

• BORN: 3/9/1912 • DIED: 8/30/1952
• PLAYED FOR TEAM: 1932 TO 1941
Joseph "Arky" Vaughan continued the team's tradition of hot-hitting shortstops. He batted better than .300 every year he was a Pirate. Vaughan's best season came in 1935, when he led the NL with a .385 average.

PIE TRAYNOR Third Baseman

- BORN: 11/11/1898 • DIED: 3/16/1972
- PLAYED FOR TEAM: 1920 TO 1935 & 1937

When Harold "Pie" Traynor joined the Pirates, most third basemen were known mainly for their fielding. Traynor was one of the first third basemen who was also a feared hitter.

PAUL WANER   Outfielder

- BORN: 4/16/1903 • DIED: 8/29/1965
- PLAYED FOR TEAM: 1926 TO 1940

Paul Waner and his brother Lloyd were two of the best outfielders in the NL. Paul won three batting championships for the Pirates. He was also a good right fielder with a powerful arm.

RALPH KINER   Outfielder

- BORN: 10/27/1922
- PLAYED FOR TEAM: 1946 TO 1953

Horseshoe-shaped Forbes Field could be a difficult park for sluggers. Ralph Kiner was able to hit balls down the left field line, where the fence was closer to home plate. Soon, that area became known as "Kiner's Korner." Kiner led the NL in home runs in his first seven seasons with the Pirates.

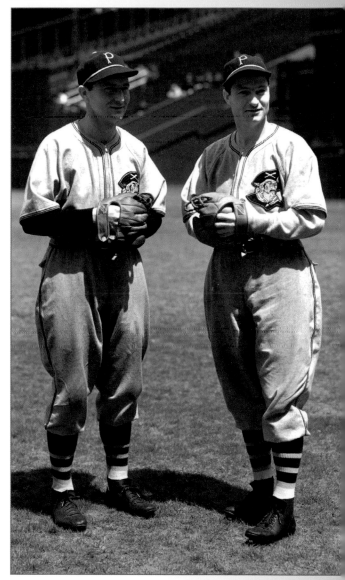

LEFT: Arky Vaughan   **ABOVE**: Paul and Lloyd Waner

21

Roberto Clemente

Printed in U.S.A.

ROBERTO CLEMENTE   Outfielder

- BORN: 8/18/1934   • DIED: 12/31/1972
- PLAYED FOR TEAM: 1955 TO 1972

Roberto Clemente played baseball with great style. He won four batting championships and 12 **Gold Gloves**—and was the league's **Most Valuable Player (MVP)** in 1966. Clemente got his 3,000th hit in the final game of his career.

BILL MAZEROSKI   Second Baseman

- BORN: 9/5/1936
- PLAYED FOR TEAM: 1956 TO 1972

Bill Mazeroski hit the home run that won the 1960 World Series, but he was best known for his defense. "Maz" rarely made an error, and no one was better at completing double plays.

WILLIE STARGELL   Outfielder/First Baseman

- BORN: 3/6/1940   • DIED: 4/9/2001   • PLAYED FOR TEAM: 1962 TO 1982

The secret to Willie Stargell's success was staying relaxed. Few players enjoyed the game more than he did. Even fewer could hit the ball as far. In 1979, at the age of 39, "Pops" was the MVP for the regular season, **National League Championship Series (NLCS)**, and World Series.

ABOVE: Roberto Clemente
RIGHT: Dave Parker

DAVE PARKER Outfielder

- BORN: 6/9/1951
- PLAYED FOR TEAM: 1973 TO 1983

Dave Parker was nicknamed the "Cobra" for the way he uncoiled his body when he swung. He was one of baseball's best all-around players, and one of the toughest. In 1978, Parker played with a broken jaw and won the NL MVP.

BARRY BONDS   Outfielder

- BORN: 7/24/1964
- PLAYED FOR TEAM: 1986 TO 1992

Barry Bonds began his career with the Pirates when he was 21. He soon became one of baseball's best players. With Pittsburgh, Bonds scored more than 100 runs twice and drove in more than 100 three times. He also won three Gold Gloves.

ANDREW McCUTCHEN Outfielder

- BORN: 10/10/1986   • FIRST YEAR WITH TEAM: 2009

In 2009, Andrew McCutchen had one of the greatest games of any Pirates rookie. He hit three home runs and drove in six runs against the Washington Nationals. In 2011, McCutchen had his first "20–20" season, with 23 homers and 23 stolen bases.

A good baseball manager tries to stay one step ahead of the manager in the other dugout. The Pirates have a special talent for finding leaders like this. Bill McKechnie guided the team from 1922 to 1926. Pittsburgh won the World Series in 1925. The Pirates never had a losing season under McKechnie. Fans used to say that he forgot more about baseball than other managers knew!

Three other managers stand out among the many good ones the Pirates have had. Danny Murtaugh managed the club four different times. He led a young team to the championship in 1960 and an experienced club to another championship in 1971. In 1979, Chuck Tanner didn't like the way his team was playing so he made several daring changes during the summer. The Pirates turned their season around and won another World Series that fall. Jim Leyland did not win any pennants in Pittsburgh, but many fans thought he was the smartest manager the Pirates ever had.

Most Pittsburgh fans have barely heard of Fred Clarke. Not only was Clarke a fine manager, he was a power-hitting outfielder, too. He did both jobs for the Pirates from 1900 to 1915. The team won four pennants during that stretch.

Clarke drove opponents crazy. He was a wild man on the bases, daring teams to throw him out. As a manager, he asked nothing less of his players. As a result, teams hated to face the Pirates. With Clarke calling the shots, there wasn't a moment they could let their guard down.

LEFT: Fred Clarke   **ABOVE**: Jim Leyland talks baseball with Andy Van Slyke. Leyland helped Van Slyke become an All-Star.

No one thought the Pirates had a chance in the 1960 World Series. The New York Yankees had some of the greatest stars in baseball. Few fans outside of Pittsburgh knew the players on the Pirates. The Yankees showed their might in their three victories.

They outscored the Pirates 38–3 in those games.

But the Pirates won three games, too. Their victories came by scores of 6–4, 3–2, and 5–2. The seventh game of the World Series was played in Pittsburgh, and it seesawed back and forth. The Pirates led 4–0 after four innings, with starting pitcher Vern Law looking strong. The Yankees came back to take the lead 5–4 in the sixth inning. They scored two more runs to make it 7–4 in the eighth.

The Pirates stormed back. A couple of lucky bounces and a home run by catcher Hal Smith put them ahead 9–7. When the ninth

LEFT: Bill Mazeroski was better known for his fielding than his hitting.
RIGHT: "Maz" heads for home after his World Series home run.

inning started, Pittsburgh needed three outs for the championship. The Yankees would not give up. They scratched out two runs to tie the score 9–9.

Bill Mazeroski, the Pirates' light-hitting second baseman, stepped into the batter's box to begin the bottom of the ninth inning. He faced Ralph Terry, a very tricky pitcher. Terry threw a fastball, and Mazeroski let it go for a ball. Terry's next pitch was high and inside. Mazeroski met the ball with the fat part of his bat and watched as his drive soared over the fence in left field.

The crowd at Forbes Field was caught off guard. They went from dead silence to mad cheering. It took Mazeroski a moment to realize that he had just won the World Series with one swing. By the time he rounded the bases, he had a wide grin on his face. Fans and teammates rushed on the field to congratulate Mazeroski as he neared home plate. It was the greatest day ever for Pittsburgh baseball.

LEGEND HAS IT

WHO WAS THE TOUGHEST PIRATE?

LEGEND HAS IT that Fred Clarke was. Clarke played hard and never complained about the bumps and bruises he got as one of the game's most *aggressive* players. After he retired from baseball, fans found out just how tough Clarke really was. He became a rancher in Kansas, one of the toughest jobs there is. Over the next few decades, Clarke fell into a lake while ice fishing, got shot in a hunting accident, and was in his house when the furnace exploded. He survived each time and lived to the age of 78.

ABOVE: Fred Clarke's picture may have been printed on silk in this image, but he was as tough as nails!

HOW DID THE PIRATES GET THEIR NAME?

LEGEND HAS IT that they "pirated" some of their players. In 1890, the Pittsburgh Alleghenys won only 23 games. The club's owners decided to dump the team and start a new one in 1891. They did this for many reasons, but mostly because it allowed the club to sign stars from other teams and leagues. Pittsburgh was later accused of taking players from their rightful owners. Soon the team became known as the Pirates.

WHICH PIRATE NEEDED ON-THE-JOB TRAINING?

LEGEND HAS IT that Neil Walker did. Walker signed a contract with the Pirates at age 18. He played catcher in high school, and that's where he started his career in the **minor leagues**. After three years, the team decided Walker would make a better third baseman. In 2010, at age 24, Walker was called up to the Pirates and told to take grounders at second base—a position where he had only played a handful of games in his life! Happy for the chance to play, Walker practiced like crazy and soon he was one of the best all-around second basemen in the league. In 2011, he had the second-best **fielding average** in the NL!

New Year's Eve is usually a time of celebration. But on December 31, 1972, baseball fans all over the world felt a deep sadness. Roberto Clemente, the Pirates' greatest player, died in an airplane crash. Clemente was on his way to deliver food and medicine to the people of Nicaragua, about 1,500 miles from his home in Puerto Rico.

Eight days earlier, a deadly earthquake had rocked Nicaragua. Clemente had many friends in the Central American country. As soon as he heard the news, he began collecting relief supplies. Three loads of cargo left Puerto Rico by plane. Unfortunately, government soldiers took the food, medicine, and other necessities soon after they arrived in Nicaragua. Clemente was very angry when he heard this news. He believed that the only way to make sure the supplies got into the right hands was to go to do the job himself. No one would dare steal from Roberto Clemente!

Clemente crammed an airplane full of new supplies and hopped on board. The plane was old and overloaded. It strained to get airborne. Once aloft, something terrible happened. The plane crashed

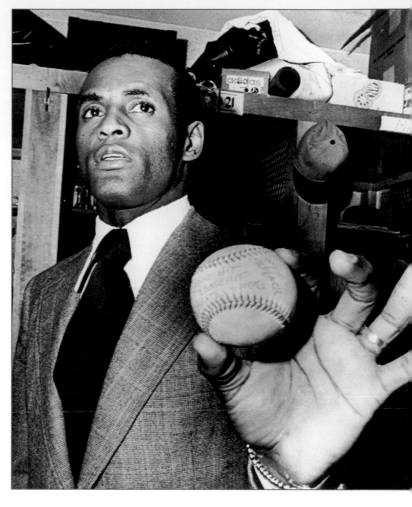

Roberto Clemente shows the ball from the 3,000th (and final) hit of his career.

into the Caribbean. Some believe that the cargo broke loose inside the aircraft and suddenly shifted. Baseball not only lost a great player. The sport lost a great person.

That spring, Clemente was voted into the **Hall of Fame**. He was only the second Latino-American to earn this honor. Normally, a Hall of Fame vote cannot take place for five years after a player's last game. But **Major League Baseball** made an exception for Clemente. The sport later started the Roberto Clemente Award, which goes to the player who best follows Clemente's example as a *humanitarian*. One more honor awaited Clemente. In 2003, his family accepted the Presidential Medal of Freedom. The medal is awarded to people who have provided great service to the country and worked for world peace.

Anyone who wants to see loyal baseballs fan should spend a day in the stands at a Pirates game. Pittsburgh fans always root hard for their team, whether the Pirates are winning or losing. They stand and cheer for the young players, even if they make a mistake or two. They let the experienced players know how much they admire their talent, too.

The Pirates show their appreciation by spending time with fans before each game. If a player sees a boy or girl waiting patiently for his autograph, he'll almost always trot over and sign his name. Once the game starts, fans have lots to do at the ballpark. There are stores, restaurants, and fun activities all over the stadium. And you never know when you might run into Captain Jolly Roger or the Pirate Parrot, Pittsburgh's team mascots.

LEFT: Jason Bay signs an autograph before the 2006 All-Star Game.
ABOVE: The Pirates and their fans have been close since Forbes Field opened in 1909. This ticket is from the first game there.

33

TIMELINE

Tommy Leach led all hitters with a .360 average in the 1909 World Series.

1902
The Pirates rule the NL with a record of 103–36.

1909
The Pirates defeat the Detroit Tigers to win the World Series.

1946
Rookie Ralph Kiner leads the NL with 23 home runs.

1887
The team joins the NL after five years in the American Association.

1927
Paul and Lloyd Waner lead the Pirates to the pennant.

1937
First baseman Gus Suhr sets an NL record by playing 822 games in a row.

Fred Dunlap was one of the team's early stars.

Gus Suhr

Kent Tekulve saved
31 games for the
Pirates in 1979.

Freddy
Sanchez

1979
The Pirates defeat
the Baltimore Orioles
in the World Series.

1990
Doug Drabek wins
the **Cy Young Award**.

2006
Freddy Sanchez wins
the batting title.

1960
The Pirates defeat the
New York Yankees in
the World Series.

1983
Bill Madlock wins
his second batting
title as a Pirate.

2011
Joel Hanrahan becomes
the third Pirate with at
least 40 **saves** in a season.

Bill
Madlock

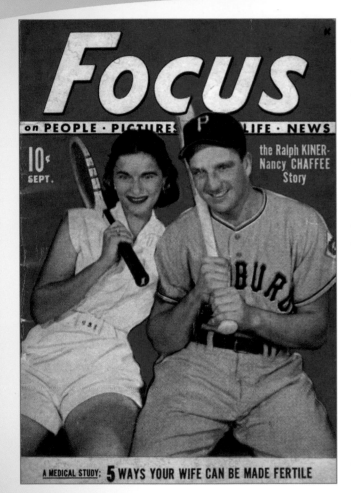

DREAMY DUO

In 1951, Ralph Kiner married tennis star Nancy Chaffee. They instantly became the "dream couple" of American sports.

HARD HATS

The Pirates were the first team to demand that their players wear batting helmets. They started using them in 1952, and other teams later did the same.

OVERSEAS SENSATIONS

In 2008, the Pirates became the first baseball team to sign a player born in India. They actually signed two—pitchers Rinku Singh and Dinesh Patel.

ABOVE: Nancy Chaffee and Ralph Kiner pose for a 1951 magazine cover.
RIGHT: Roy Face led the NL in saves three times.

In Your Face

Roy Face was the best relief pitcher of his day. He won 22 games in a row in 1958 and 1959, and saved three games in the 1960 World Series. Face's best weapon was a sinking pitch called a forkball.

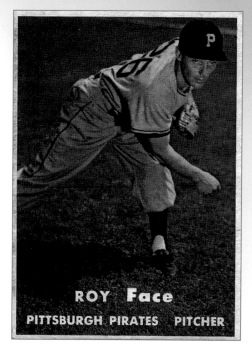

ROY Face
PITTSBURGH PIRATES   PITCHER

Isn't It Grand?

In 1956, Roberto Clemente hit an inside-the-park home run with the bases loaded in the bottom of the ninth inning to win a game against the Chicago Cubs. It was the first time anyone had done this in big-league history.

Sharing the Glory

In 1997, Francisco Cordova and Ricardo Rincon teamed up to pitch a **no-hitter** against the Houston Astros in 10 innings. It was the first time two pitchers did this in a game that lasted more than nine innings.

5 + 5 = 40

In 2010, Andrew McCutchen and Garrett Jones each had five hits in the same game. The last Pittsburgh teammates to do that were Willie Stargell and Bob Robertson—40 years earlier.

"When I put on my uniform, I feel I am the proudest man on Earth."

▶ **ROBERTO CLEMENTE**, *ON PLAYING RIGHT FIELD FOR THE PIRATES*

TOPPS 2010
ALL-STAR
ROOKIE

NEIL
WALKER
PITTSBURGH PIRATES® 2B

"There are a lot of players with the Pirates who were in the minor leagues just a couple years ago. It's definitely a good *incentive* to work hard and see where it takes you."

▶ **NEIL WALKER**, *ON HOW THE TEAM TRIES TO BUILD A WINNER*

"After it was over, it was pretty much like any other game. I just thought it was another home run to win a ballgame."

▶ **BILL MAZEROSKI**, *ON HIS HOME RUN THAT WON THE 1960 WORLD SERIES*

"Pittsburgh isn't fancy, but it is real. I feel as much a part of this city as the cobblestone streets and the steel mills."

▶ **WILLIE STARGELL**, *ON WHY HE LOVED PITTSBURGH*

"I don't make speeches. I just let my bat speak for me in the summertime."

▶ **HONUS WAGNER**, *ON BEING A QUIET LEADER*

HONUS WAGNER

"Parker gave 100 percent effort in every inning of every game that he played. He was one of the greatest I ever managed and one of the greatest who ever played."

▶ **CHUCK TANNER**, *ON DAVE PARKER, THE 1978 NL MVP*

"He had the quickest hands and the quickest arms of any third baseman I ever saw."

▶ **CHARLIE GRIMM**, *ON TEAMMATE PIE TRAYNOR, WHO WAS ELECTED TO THE HALL OF FAME IN 1948*

LEFT: Neil Walker
RIGHT: Honus Wagner

GREAT DEBATES

People who root for the Pirates love to compare their favorite moments, teams, and players. Some debates have been going on for years! How would you settle these classic baseball arguments?

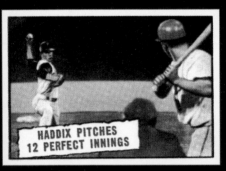

HADDIX PITCHES
12 PERFECT INNINGS

HARVEY HADDIX PITCHED THE GREATEST GAME IN TEAM HISTORY ...

… because he got 36 outs in a row against the Milwaukee Braves in 1959. Pitching a **perfect game** for nine innings is a rare achievement. Throwing 12 perfect innings had never been done before. No one has done it since. In fact, no one has even come close. Haddix (LEFT) was so good that the Braves fans stood and cheered for him after each inning.

THAT WOULD BE NEWS TO STEVE BLASS ...

… because he pitched the best game of his life in Game 7 of the 1971 World Series, with the championship on the line. Blass faced the power-packed Baltimore Orioles. Their lineup led the American League in hitting that year. Blass allowed only four hits in nine innings. He threw so hard that his cap kept flying off his head. Oh, one other thing. Blass won his game 2–1. Haddix gave up a home run in the 13th inning and lost.

WILLIE STARGELL WAS PITTSBURGH'S GREATEST POWER HITTER ...

… because he could hit the ball a mile. Stargell (RIGHT) blasted some of the longest homers in history. A couple traveled more than 500 feet. He hit the only ball ever to reach the upper deck of Olympic Stadium in Montreal. That ball was measured at 535 feet. Stargell hit 475 home runs for the Pirates and led the NL in long balls twice. In 2011, the U.S. Postal Service announced that it was honoring Stargell (who died in 2001) with a new stamp. "I'm sure he's looking down and smiling," his wife said.

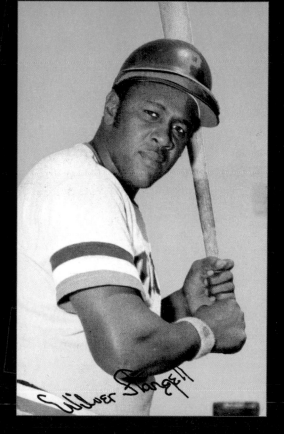

SORRY, BUT RALPH KINER WINS THIS BATTLE ...

… because the way you measure power hitting is with home run crowns. Kiner was the NL's home run champ every year from 1946 to 1952—seven years in a row. Not even Babe Ruth did that! Kiner was a very patient hitter. He would wait for a pitch he could hit down the left field line and into the seats. Not surprisingly, Kiner also led the NL in walks three times. He had 100 or more six years in a row.

FOR THE RECORD

The great Pirates teams and players have left their marks on the record books. These are the "best of the best" …

Dick Groat

PIRATES AWARD WINNERS

WINNER	AWARD	YEAR
Vern Law	Cy Young Award	1960
Dick Groat	Most Valuable Player	1960
Roberto Clemente	Most Valuable Player	1966
Roberto Clemente	World Series MVP	1971
Dave Parker	Most Valuable Player	1978
Dave Parker	All-Star Game MVP	1979
Willie Stargell	co-Most Valuable Player	1979
Willie Stargell	World Series MVP	1979
Jim Leyland	Manager of the Year	1990
Doug Drabek	Cy Young Award	1990
Barry Bonds	Most Valuable Player	1990
Jim Leyland	Manager of the Year	1992
Barry Bonds	Most Valuable Player	1992
Jason Bay	Rookie of the Year*	2004

• *The award given to each league's best first-year player.*

Jim Leyland

This postcard shows Forbes Field right after it opened in 1909.

PIRATES ACHIEVEMENTS

ACHIEVEMENT	YEAR
NL Pennant Winners	1901
NL Pennant Winners	1902
NL Pennant Winners	1903
NL Pennant Winners	1909
World Series Champions	1909
NL Pennant Winners	1925
World Series Champions	1925
NL Pennant Winners	1927
NL Pennant Winners	1960
World Series Champions	1960
NL East Champions	1970
NL East Champions	1971
NL Pennant Winners	1971
World Series Champions	1971
NL East Champions	1972
NL East Champions	1974
NL East Champions	1975
NL East Champions	1979
NL Pennant Winners	1979
World Series Champions	1979
NL East Champions	1990
NL East Champions	1991
NL East Champions	1992

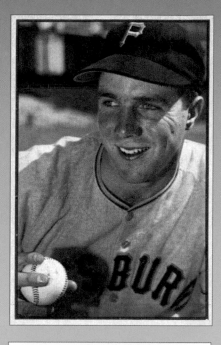

PHIL GARNER

TOP: Bob Friend led the 1960 champs in strikeouts.
ABOVE: Phil Garner played three positions for the 1979 Pirates.
LEFT: This rare pin shows the 1902 club.

43

PINPOINTS

The history of a baseball team is made up of many smaller stories. These stories take place all over the map—not just in the city a team calls "home." Match the pushpins on these maps to the **TEAM FACTS**, and you will begin to see the story of the Pirates unfold!

1 Pittsburgh, Pennsylvania—*The Pirates have played here since 1883.*

2 Baltimore, Maryland—*The Pirates won the 1971 World Series here.*

3 Boston, Massachusetts—*The Pirates played in the first World Series here.*

4 Cincinnati, Ohio—*Kent Tekulve was born here.*

5 Memphis, Tennessee—*Bill Madlock was born here.*

6 Winterset, Iowa—*Fred Clarke was born here.*

7 Meridian, Idaho—*Vern Law was born here.*

8 Earlsboro, Oklahoma—*Willie Stargell was born here.*

9 San Diego, California—*Jason Kendall was born here.*

10 Trail, British Columbia, Canada—*Jason Bay was born here*

11 Colon, Panama—*Manny Sanguillen was born here.*

12 Bhadohi, Uttar Pradesh, India—*Rinku Singh was born here.*

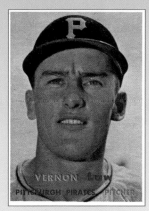

Vern Law

GLOSSARY

🧠 *AGGRESSIVE*—Acting boldly or powerfully.

🧠 **ALL-STARS**—Players who are selected to play in baseball's annual All-Star Game.

🧠 **AMERICAN ASSOCIATION (AA)**—A rival to the National League in the 1800s. The AA played from 1882 to 1891.

🧠 **AMERICAN LEAGUE (AL)**—One of baseball's two major leagues; the AL began play in 1901.

🧠 **CY YOUNG AWARD**—The award given each year to each league's best pitchers.

🧠 *DECADE*—A period of 10 years; also specific periods, such as the 1950s.

🧠 **FIELDING AVERAGE**—A statistic that measures a player's defensive ability.

🧠 *GENERATIONS*—Periods of years roughly equal to the time it takes for a person to be born, grow up, and have children.

🧠 **GOLD GLOVES**—The awards given each year to baseball's best fielders.

🧠 **HALL OF FAME**—The museum in Cooperstown, New York, where baseball's greatest players are honored. A player voted into the Hall of Fame is sometimes called a "Hall of Famer."

🧠 *HUMANITARIAN*—Someone devoted to making life better for people in difficult situations.

🧠 *INCENTIVE*—Something that pushes a person to work harder.

🧠 **MAJOR LEAGUE BASEBALL**—The top level of professional baseball leagues. The AL and NL make up today's major leagues. Sometimes called the big leagues.

🧠 **MINOR LEAGUES**—The many professional leagues that help develop players for the major leagues.

🧠 **MOST VALUABLE PLAYER (MVP)**—The award given each year to each league's top player; an MVP is also selected for the World Series and the All-Star Game.

🧠 **NATIONAL LEAGUE (NL)**—The older of the two major leagues; the NL began play in 1876.

🧠 **NATIONAL LEAGUE CHAMPIONSHIP SERIES (NLCS)**—The playoff series that has decided the National League pennant since 1969.

🧠 **NL CENTRAL**—A group of National League teams that play in the central part of the country.

🧠 **NO-HITTER**—A game in which a team does not get a hit.

🧠 **PENNANT**—A league championship. The term comes from the triangular flag awarded to each season's champion, beginning in the 1870s.

🧠 **PERFECT GAME**—A game in which no batter reaches base.

🧠 *PINSTRIPES*—Thin stripes.

🧠 **PLAYER-MANAGER**—A player who also manages his team.

🧠 **ROOKIE**—A player in his first season.

🧠 **RUNS BATTED IN (RBIs)**—A statistic that counts the number of runners a batter drives home.

🧠 **SAVES**—A statistic that counts the number of times a relief pitcher finishes off a close victory for his team.

🧠 *TRADITION*—A belief or custom that is handed down from generation to generation.

🧠 **WORLD SERIES**—The world championship series played between the AL and NL pennant winners.

EXTRA INNINGS

TEAM SPIRIT introduces a great way to stay up to date with your team! Visit our **EXTRA INNINGS** link and get connected to the latest and greatest updates. **EXTRA INNINGS** serves as a young reader's ticket to an exclusive web page—with more stories, fun facts, team records, and photos of the Pirates. Content is updated during and after each season. The **EXTRA INNINGS** feature also enables readers to send comments and letters to the author! Log onto:

www.norwoodhousepress.com/library.aspx

and click on the tab: **TEAM SPIRIT** to access **EXTRA INNINGS**.

Read all the books in the series to learn more about professional sports. For a complete listing of the baseball, basketball, football, and hockey teams in the **TEAM SPIRIT** series, visit our website at:

www.norwoodhousepress.com/library.aspx

ON THE ROAD

PITTSBURGH PIRATES
115 Federal Street
Pittsburgh, Pennsylvania 15212
(412) 321-2827
pittsburgh.pirates.mlb.com

**NATIONAL BASEBALL
HALL OF FAME AND MUSEUM**
25 Main Street
Cooperstown, New York 13326
(888) 425-5633
www.baseballhalloffame.org

ON THE BOOKSHELF

To learn more about the sport of baseball, look for these books at your library or bookstore:

• Augustyn, Adam (editor). *The Britannica Guide to Baseball*. New York, NY: Rosen Publishing, 2011.

• Dreier, David. *Baseball: How It Works*. North Mankato, MN: Capstone Press, 2010.

• Stewart, Mark. *Ultimate 10: Baseball*. New York, NY: Gareth Stevens Publishing, 2009.

ABOUT THE AUTHOR

PAGE NUMBERS IN **BOLD** REFER TO ILLUSTRATIONS.

MARK STEWART has written more than 50 books on baseball and over 150 sports books for kids. He grew up in New York City during the 1960s rooting for the Yankees and Mets, and was lucky enough to meet players from both teams. Mark comes from a family of writers. His grandfather was Sunday Editor of *The New York Times,* and his mother was Articles Editor of *Ladies' Home Journal* and *McCall's*. Mark has profiled hundreds of athletes over the past 25 years. He has also written several books about his native New York and New Jersey, his home today. Mark is a graduate of Duke University, with a degree in history. He lives and works in a home overlooking Sandy Hook, New Jersey. You can contact Mark through the Norwood House Press website.